Spotlight on Equine Nutrition Series

Equine Digestion

It's Decidedly Different

Juliet M. Getty, Ph.D.

Equine Digestion: It's Decidedly Different was transcribed and expanded from a teleseminar presented by Dr. Juliet M. Getty.

Transcription by Darlene J. Backer, CMT (DarleneJBacker@gmail.com).

Illustrations by Robin Peterson, DVM, FernWood Studio, Washington State (www.fernwoodstudio.com)

Book design, editing and publication preparation by Elizabeth Testa (DurangoEditor@gmail.com).

ISBN-13: 978-1493544622

ISBN-10: 1493544624

Printed in the United States of America

Preface & Disclaimer

Equine Digestion: It's Decidedly Different is based on a teleseminar on the subject given by Dr. Juliet M. Getty, with materials added to enhance the reader's understanding of the horse's digestive system. Dr. Getty's goal is to provide a useful, in-depth resource for anyone who wants to feed his or her horse in sync with the animal's own physiology and instincts, and thereby give the horse the optimal opportunity to enjoy a life of vibrant health.

Dr. Getty makes every effort to present the most accurate and helpful information based on her expertise and on the most reliable sources. She, her editor, transcriptionist, illustrator and publisher take no responsibility for any results or damages that might be obtained from the reliance on the information and recommendations made in this book. Furthermore, the group collectively and individually takes no responsibility for the inherent risks of activities involving horses, including equine behavior changes that might result in personal injury.

Advice about nutrition, especially in the case of illness, injury, disorders, or conditions requiring medical treatment, is not intended to take the place of proper veterinary care. It may be used in conjunction with such care to facilitate healing and maintain health. The information provided by Getty Equine Nutrition, LLC is presented for the purpose of educating horse owners. Suggested feeds, supplements, and procedures are administered voluntarily with the understanding that any adverse reaction is the responsibility of the owner. Furthermore, Getty Equine Nutrition, LLC cannot be held accountable for a horse's response, whether favorable or adverse, to nutritional intervention.

This is not a verbatim transcript. Comments about technical matters relevant to the teleseminar process have been omitted, along with questions and answers off the specific topic at hand.

Mention of a specific product or brand name is not intended to imply that other companies offer inferior products. Dr. Getty means no intention of

Juliet M. Getty, Ph.D. is an internationally respected writer and lecturer on equine nutrition. She contributes articles frequently to various horse journals and media, and her comprehensive reference book, *Feed Your Horse Like a Horse*, has educated countless horsemen and women in the science behind sound equine feeding practices.

Dr. Getty is available for private consultations and speaking engagements., and her informative e-newsletter, *Forage for Thought*, is read by several thousand subscribers every month. The *Spotlight on Equine Nutrition Series* offers these additional titles:

Aging Horse—*Helping Him Grow Old with Dignity and in Health*
Easy Keeper—*Making It Easy to Keep Him Healthy*
Equine Cushing's Disease—*Nutritional Management*
Joint Health—*A Nutritional Perspective*
Laminitis—*A Scientific and Realistic Approach*
Whole Foods & Alternative Feeds

Dr. Getty offers a generous serving of other equine nutrition knowledge at www.GettyEquineNutrition.com.

Spotlight on Equine Nutrition Series

Equine Digestion

It's Decidedly Different

Juliet M. Getty, Ph.D.

Introduction

Equine Digestion: It's Decidedly Different is about a very basic and very important topic: how your horse is designed on the inside. In other words, we're going to look at his digestive tract, and you'll find that it's just plain different.

I commend your interest in this topic. So many aspects of horse health depend on the horse's "person" understanding what makes the horse do and eat the things that he does.

What is a horse, digestively speaking? The horse is a non-ruminant herbivore, whose anatomy combines the physiology of a monogastric animal with that of a ruminant. In order to understand what this means, we need to look at other species. Let's start with the cow.

The ruminant cow

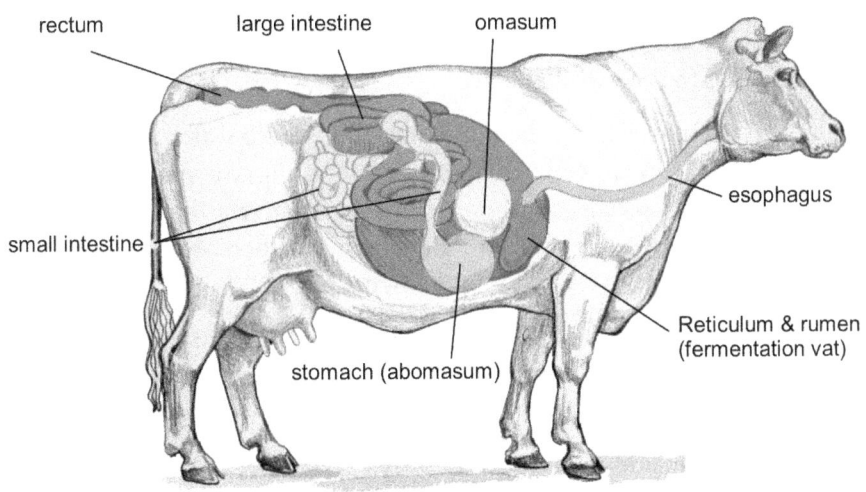

BOVINE DIGESTIVE SYSTEM

The cow is a ruminant. Examples of other ruminants are goats, sheep, giraffes, llamas, alpacas, deer, moose, and yaks – and there are more.

Notice that the cow's stomach is in four compartments—rumen, reticulum, omasum, and abomasum. The first portion, the largest, is the rumen; hence, the cow is a *ruminant*. Food is swished back and forth between the rumen and the reticulum, working together to create a huge fermentation vat, which, in the cow, contains about 32 gallons of volume and billions and billions of bacteria and other microbes that digest the fiber that is in the forage that the cow eats.

Ruminating means to chew on to something. When the cow eats some hay or grass, she chews it and swallows it. It goes into the rumen where it starts the digestion of fiber. Then she actually regurgitates it. It comes back up into her mouth, she chews it again to create more surface area, and then swallows it again. Now it's digested yet again, and this goes on for about 30% of her day; a given food will circulate between the two points for anywhere from 24 to 48 hours. We call it chewing the cud. She regurgitates it, chews it, swallows it; regurgitates it, chews it, and swallows it. So you can appreciate that this fiber is thoroughly digested; the cow benefits from everything she has eaten. The microbes ferment fibers into volatile fatty acids which are absorbed into the bloodstream, directly from the rumen, to provide energy for the cow.

The undigested material passes to the omasum, where water and minerals are absorbed, leaving something called chyme, a slurry containing undigested nutrients, to enter the last portion of the stomach, the abomasum. The abomasum is like our stomach; it contains hydrochloric acid (HCl) and pepsin (an enzyme) to start protein digestion.

The rest of the digestive tract consists of the small and large intestine, which is very much like ours. What does not get digested and absorbed is excreted into the manure.

Next, we'll look inside our human digestive system.

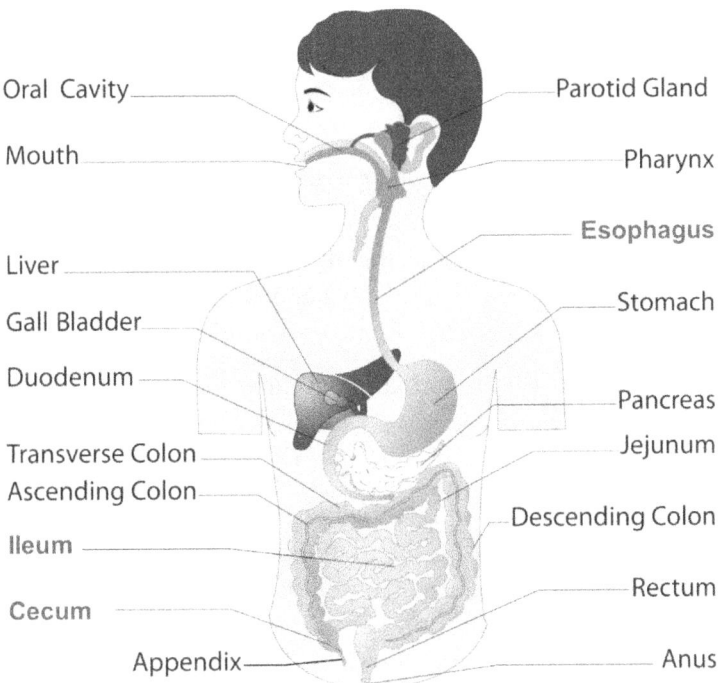

HUMAN DIGESTIVE SYSTEM

The monogastric human

We are considered monogastric since we have only one stomach. We are not ruminants because we do not have a rumen. Furthermore, we do not have a functioning fermentation vat of any kind that digests fiber. We eat fiber, not to provide calories (as with the cow) but to exercise our digestive tract's muscles; hence we can prevent "flabby" intestines from developing weakened areas, or outpouchings, a condition known as diverticulosis.

Starting with the mouth, chewing increases the food's surface area to prepare for digestion. Saliva provides lubrication for swallowing but it also contains salivary amylase, which starts starch digestion. Once swallowed, chewed food passes through a muscular opening called the lower esopha-geal sphincter (sometimes referred to as the cardiac sphincter) to enter the stomach. The stomach's acidic environment stops carbohydrate digestion (which will resume later).

In the stomach, food is exposed to HCl to denature (relax and open) long protein molecules, to facilitate enzymatic digestion. HCl also activates an enzyme called pepsin which starts the digestion of protein, breaking it down to small chains of amino acids. No appreciable amount of fat diges-tion takes place in the stomach.

The stomach is also highly muscular, with three distinct bands of muscles designed to mix and churn food into what ends up as an acid-containing slurry called "acid chyme."

Acid chyme leaves the stomach through another muscular opening called the pyloric sphincter, and enters the first section of the small intestine, the duodenum. The small intestine consists of three parts – duodenum, jeju-num, and ileum. Most digestion and absorption takes place in the first two areas, while whatever is remaining will likely get absorbed from the ileum before it reaches the large intestine.

A lot of things take place in the duodenum.

Digestion requires digestive enzymes, which are produced by the small intestine and the pancreas. However, these enzymes do not work when ac-id is present because enzymes are proteins, and acid destroys (denatures) proteins. (Even pepsin eventually becomes denatured in the stomach.) To neutralize the acid, the pancreas first floods the duodenum with sodium bicarbonate, an antacid–and yes, it's the same as baking soda!

Now that the acid chyme is no longer acidic, the digestive enzymes can do their job. They break down short protein chains into individual amino ac-ids, carbohydrates (sugars and starches) into individual single units (mostly glucose but some fructose which eventually gets converted to glu-cose in the liver), and fat (triglycerides) into its individual components—glycerol and fatty acids.

Amino acids (from protein digestion) and simple sugars called monosaccharides (from carbohydrate digestion) are absorbed from the small intestine through the portal vein to the liver. There they are utilized or shipped out into the bloodstream, according to the body's need.

Fat is more complicated. Suffice it to say that glycerol and fatty acids are "reconstructed" into triglycerides that fulfill our cell's needs. They are packaged into lipoproteins called chylomicrons and shipped to the liver, where they are repackaged with cholesterol and phospholipids into different lipoproteins, which eventually will reach the tissues.

What remains is undigested or unabsorbed material which enters the large intestine. This part of the digestive tract is responsible for the absorption of water and minerals into the bloodstream, and compacting fecal waste. Much of the material in the large intestine is in the form of fiber. Humans do not have the capability of digesting fiber. Although there are beneficial microbes within the large intestine that can digest some of it, the digestion products are not absorbed into the bloodstream so we do not benefit from fiber as a nutrient source. Instead, fiber exercises our muscles and retains fluid to help prevent disorders such as hemorrhoids and constipation.

At the base of the small intestine, on the lower right side of the abdomen, there exists a small digestive remnant called the appendix. This small organ may contain some bacteria to re-populate the intestines should the existing bacteria die off (as with antibiotics, for example). However, it is not involved in fiber digestion. In addition, in between the small and large intestine, next to the appendix, lies an area known as the cecum. It is not a fermentation vat (as we'll see later with the horse), but is instead involved in absorbing water and minerals remaining after completion of small intestinal digestion.

Another monogastric, the canine

Much like humans, dogs are another example of a monogastric animal. We have a lot of similarities with dogs, especially our inability to digest fiber and a tiny area called a cecum that has no fiber-digesting properties. But there are a few noteworthy differences.

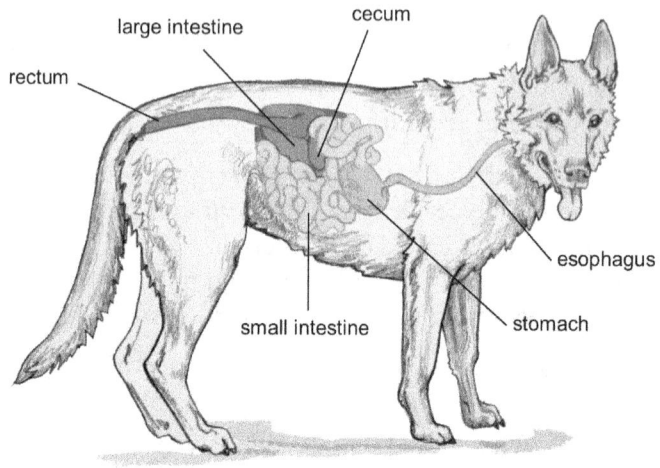

CANINE DIGESTIVE SYSTEM

- Dogs cannot grind their food; they use their molars to crush food but do not chew like we do. Therefore they can swallow large pieces of food and rely on the rest of the gastrointestinal tract for digestion. If they swallow too large a piece they simply throw it up.

- Dog's saliva contains no digestive enzymes.

- Their stomach contains more acid, allowing high protein meals to be adequately digested, which is appropriate for the carnivores they are.

I spent time going into what a horse is not, in order to appreciate what he is. He is a combination of monogastric animal with some of the fiber fermentation capability of a ruminant.

I say *some* of the fiber fermentation capability of a ruminant because the horse does not have a large fermentation vat at the beginning of his digestive tract. He cannot spend much of his day digesting fiber. Instead, the horse has a smaller fermentation vat called the cecum, very much like the rumen, at the end of the digestive tract. Because it's at the end and he cannot continuously digest and re-digest and re-digest the food, the horse's fiber digestion is rather inefficient, so he needs to have far more hay or forage available than, for example, a cow would. You can't feed a horse like a cow, or vice versa.

We'll cover the horse's digestive system in greater detail in Chapter One.

If you take the front of a dog's digestive system and at the end of it you put the front of a cow's digestive system, you kind of have what a horse looks like—a very unusual creature.[1] Not understanding the unique digestive physiology of the horse is most often the root cause of feeding errors, leading to all kinds of digestive problems that can affect the entire body.

Horses that live in a wild or natural setting have access to grass and other forage all the time, 24 hours a day, and they eat far more than just grasses. They eat leaves and flowers and weeds and brambles and nuts and berries and tree bark and all kinds of things that give them variety, that give them different types of nutrients, that give them the vitamins and minerals they need. On top of that, they walk around a lot. So, unlike our domesticated horses confined to small areas and fed a few "square" meals a day, usually of a single type of forage, wild horses don't develop the digestive disorders such as colic, ulcers, and chronic diarrhea that we see in domesticated horses; the type of laminitis that occurs as a result of these problems or from excessive consumption of sugar and starch is also not seen.

My goal with this book is to help prevent these problems by explaining the function and form of the digestive tract and to show you how to feed in sync with the way your horse is made. I don't cover specific problems such as colic or ulcers in any detail except to mention here and there how to prevent them through a deeper understanding of how horses are made on the inside. The information in this book will empower you to make the right choices for your horse by yourself and not to rely on your neighbor or the feed store clerk or "conventional wisdom" or even traditional practices. You will know the right way to feed and you'll be able to talk knowledgeably to those in whose care you may place your horse.

Many barn managers, for example, prioritize the bottom line over the horse's welfare, but their restrictive feeding practices may be detrimental to the horse's health. They even may scare the horse owners into thinking that feeding hay free choice, for example, will get their horses fat, or their horses will colic or develop a host of other problems. In this book, I hope to give you the knowledge you need to help yourself and to help your horses.

So, let's go ahead and begin our journey. Along the way, I'll give you pointers on how to prevent problems and at the end we'll conclude with the right way to feed horses forage free- choice. By that point, I sincerely hope you will understand why the best feeding practice is the one that respects the horse's own physiology.

Chapter One: Digestive Organs of the Horse

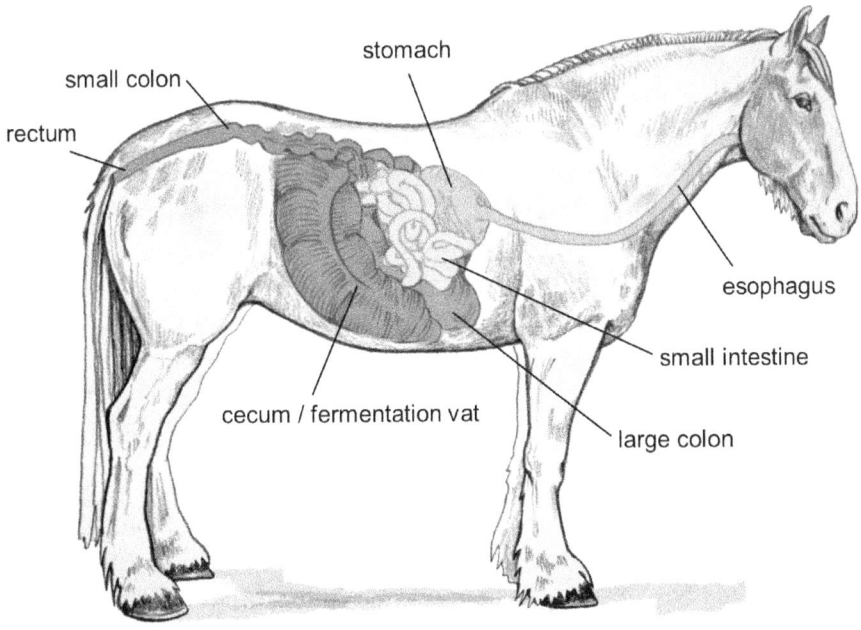

EQUINE DIGESTIVE SYSTEM

Touring the horse's digestive tract

We're going to travel from the mouth to the esophagus to the stomach to the small intestine (the foregut), and then we're going into the cecum, the large colon, the small colon and the rectum.

Mouth and esophagus

We start in the mouth where, obviously, the horse chews. Horses need their molars to chew and grind coarse fibrous plants into manageable pieces. Doing so increases the surface area of the food so that by the time it gets to the stomach and the small intestine, the digestive enzymes are better able to extract the available nutrients.

Another very important aspect of chewing is saliva production. In horses, food must be present in the mouth to stimulate saliva flow; there is no influence from psychological stimulation, as we encounter, for example, when we see delicious food. Your horse produces great amounts of saliva, about 12 quarts per day on average, depending on what he's eating. Hay, for example, causes twice the saliva production as grain does. (Note, when I say grain, I mean a cereal grain or any feeds that contain cereal grains such as oats, corn, and barley.[3]) When grains and grain mixes are chewed very quickly, they're swallowed in about ten minutes, whereas a horse can chew on hay for about twice as much time, maybe even three times, all the while creating saliva, which lubricates the feed and also functions as a natural antacid. When we discuss the stomach, you'll understand better the importance of saliva. But before we get to the stomach, let's talk about the esophagus.

The esophagus is really nothing more than a long tube. It's about 4-5 feet in length and its only purpose is to conduct food from the mouth to the stomach. At the base of the esophagus is the same strong esophageal sphincter that we see in humans and other monogastrics. However, it is very well formed in the horse and it closes really, really tightly. It enters the stomach at an oblique angle which is why horses cannot vomit unless it's a very serious situation; they can't belch either. In fact, they generally cannot expel any gas through the esophagus unless something (such as an ulcer) compromises the sphincter's strength.

Stomach

We've arrived now at the stomach. The stomach is divided into two basic areas. One area of the horse's stomach, the glandular area at the base, is protected from stomach acid by producing copious amounts of mucus. The other portion, the squamous region, has no mucous lining for protection—this is where ulcers tend to form most often.

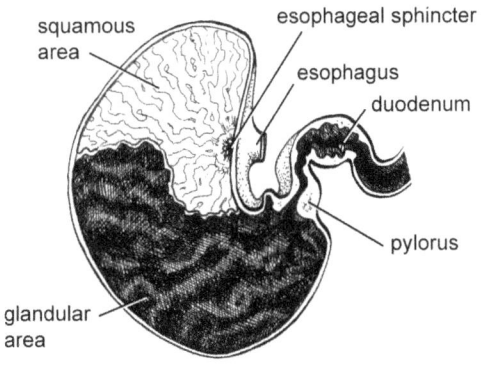

THE EQUINE STOMACH

Te stomach is rather small compared to the rest of the digestive tract. It's ohnly about 2-4 gallons in size; that's really tiny compared to the rest of the digestive tract, so I recommend that you don't feed more than four pounds of any feed at a time, depending on the size of the horse. Four pounds is a measurement of weight, not volume. Remember, scoops don't measure weight; they measure volume. You have 2-quart scoops, 3-quart scoops, 4-quart scoops. Quarts are volume measurements. If you fill a 2-quart scoop with oats and weigh it, it'll probably weigh about three pounds. If you fill it with beet pulp, it'll weigh only one pound. The only way to be certain of the amount you're feeding is to get yourself a scale, weigh the feed in the scoop and mark it for future reference relative to that particular feed. If you don't have a scale, consider taking the scoop and the feed to the grocery store to use the scales in the produce department.

The most important fact to grasp about the horse's stomach is that it produces acid all the time, whether or not it contains food to digest. When you eat, your stomach produces acid, but when you stop eating, your stomach stops producing acid and you are comfortable. In the horse, this is not the case. Even if the horse has an empty stomach, acid is produced anyway.

This is where the all-important saliva comes in. Saliva that the horse swallows neutralizes the acid, thereby helping prevent the formation of ulcers in that upper squamous region. Your horse needs to be able to eat all the time so the saliva will do its necessary work and so the food itself will soak up the acid. Otherwise the acid sits in the empty stomach.

This mechanism is the reason horses are trickle feeders. They're meant to be able to graze 24 hours a day.

This also has bearing on feeding before exercise. Think for a moment about a very common scenario with your horse. The horse has an empty stomach, there's acid in there, and you take him out to exercise. You ask him to move, maybe you ask him to run, and so he does, and what happens to that acid? It sloshes around and ends up hitting the unprotected upper area of the stomach, causing ulcers. This is why you should never exercise a horse without feeding him some forage—not grain—first. (In fact, he should always have forage available, but we'll get to the details of that later.) This is why 90-95% of all race and other speed event horses and about 50% of all performance horses have ulcers—their owners or trainers make this one critical mistake: They don't allow the horse to have forage in the stomach during exercise.

Now what is the purpose of this acid and how does it work? You may think it's a nuisance. Actually, it's not. The acid (which is HCl) has a couple of functions. First of all, it is part of the horse's immune function, his first line of defense against any microbial pathogens he may pick up when he eats off the ground. Acid's second function is to activate the enzyme pepsin which starts the digestion of protein. Without enough acid, protein digestion is not started and therefore the horse may not get all of the amino acid that he needs to build body tissues. Since the horse's diet does not contain meat (as with the dog, for example) the pH of the stomach does not need to be very low (acidic) but just low enough to start the activation of pepsin.

For these reasons, I am against feeding antacids on a regular basis. Antacids or H2 blockers or proton pump inhibitors such omeprazole have short-term applications; they should not be fed long term because they either neutralize or completely turn off the horse's acid-making machinery–a very harmful outcome.

Also, we now know that there are bacteria in the stomach that can produce volatile fatty acids which increase the acid in the stomach when starch is present, so if you feed a lot of starchy feed (e.g., cereal grains), the bacteria produce acids from it. They also can produce a lot of gas (which, remember, cannot escape up the esophagus), so a large meal with a lot of starch can actually lead to stomach rupture.

What you feed can influence gastric emptying time. I'm often asked, "Should I feed hay or grain first?" Well, the true answer is that hay (or fresh pasture) should always be available and present in the digestive tract. But if your horse should happen to have an empty stomach, it is best to feed hay first. Starchy feeds quickly leave the stomach, leaving it exposed to acid. If hay is present, it will slow down the passage of starch into the small intestine, thereby allowing more complete digestion. Inadequately digested starch can end up in the hindgut where its fermentation can lead to problems.

The stomach is a very powerful organ. Just as we saw with monogastric animals, the horse's stomach is made of three different bands of muscles that mix and churn the food into a semi-liquid mass called chyme. After about an hour the chyme is ready to leave the stomach and enter the small intestine. The pyloric sphincter separates the stomach from the small intestine's first section (duodenum) and generally prevents chyme from flowing back inside the stomach. However, when the stomach is empty, this is more likely to occur, potentially leading to stomach or duodenal ulcers.

Onward to the gastrointestinal tract. See illustration, following page.

The small intestine

The small intestine is quite long—approximately 60 to 70 feet—and holds about 12 gallons, far more volume than the stomach. It is comprised of three sections – the duodenum, jejunum, and ileum.

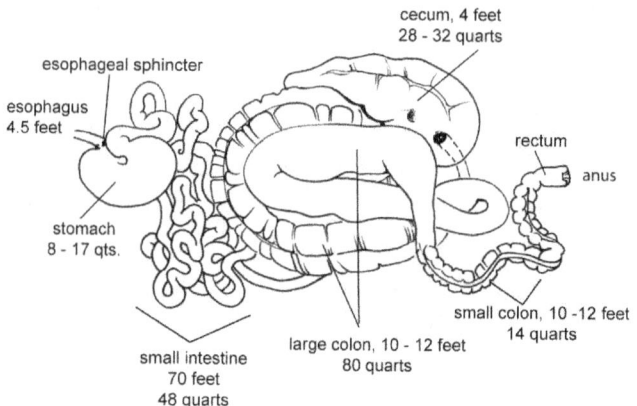

cecum, 4 feet
28 - 32 quarts

esophageal sphincter

esophagus
4.5 feet

rectum

anus

stomach
8 - 17 qts.

small colon, 10 -12 feet
14 quarts

large colon, 10 - 12 feet
80 quarts

small intestine
70 feet
48 quarts

THE EQUINE GASTROINTESTINAL TRACT

The digestive process that occurs in the horse's small intestine is very much the same as in other mammals, both monogastric and ruminant. Bile is produced by the liver and enters the duodenum via the bile duct. Sodium bicarbonate and digestive enzymes from the pancreas are released into the duodenum via the pancreatic duct. Bile facilitates fat digestion but first, the acid chyme from the stomach must be neutralized (the pH must be raised) through the action of sodium bicarbonate so that digestive enzymes can function.

Digestive enzymes (sucrase, maltase, lipase and peptidases) are also secreted from the duodenal cells to digest the nutrients in the food matter. In fact, all the non-structural nutrients (sugars, starches, proteins, and fats) the horse gets are digested in the small intestine.

In the case of forage, fiber cannot be digested in the small intestine; it has to get digested by the hindgut bacteria because the enzymes that are needed to digest fiber are not found in the small intestine or the pancreas. We'll come to that further along. We're going to discuss carbohydrates, proteins, and fats first.

Carbohydrates

Carbohydrates in the form of starch are long, branched molecules that the body needs to break down into individual glucose molecules. The enzyme that does that is called amylase, and it is produced by the pancreas. However, in the horse the pancreas does not produce a lot of amylase. Why? Because the horse is not designed to digest a lot of starch. It just isn't made that way.

So when you feed a horse a large amount of starch, much of it can go undigested. Then what happens? It can end up in the hindgut where it can be fermented, creating endotoxins which can lead to laminitis.

The starch that does get digested is broken down to glucose, a monosaccharide (simple sugar). Glucose is the predominant blood sugar and is quickly absorbed into the bloodstream. When the blood glucose concentration rises it signals the pancreas to secrete the hormone insulin. Insulin's job is to take the glucose out of the blood and allow it to enter into the tissues. If you feed a lot of starch and end up with a lot of glucose in the blood stream, that leads to a lot of insulin; when insulin goes up, it causes inflammation in the foot which can lead to laminitis. If you are concerned about your horse having laminitis or being at risk for laminitis, whether it be from insulin resistance or from equine Cushing's disease, I highly recommend you study my books on Laminitis or Cushing's, part of the growing *Spotlight on Equine Nutrition Series.*[4]

Sugar is often added to horse feeds in the form of molasses. This molecule is actually a disaccharide—a combination of two monosaccharides, glucose and fructose, linked together. Since it is too large to be absorbed, it is digested down to individual simple sugars. In the liver, fructose is largely converted to glucose. So, even fructose from fruit contributes to the overall blood glucose level.

Fiber is also considered a carbohydrate, though it is indigestible at this stage within the gastrointestinal tract. More on fiber later.

Protein

Proteins are very large molecules consisting of 100 or more amino acids linked together in specific sequences. They are digested by proteases, enzymes capable of breaking these large molecules down to the individual amino acids. These are then absorbed into the blood stream and reassembled within each cell to make body proteins. So, if the amino acids go into liver cells, they make liver proteins; if they go into skin cells, they make skin proteins, etc. This is called differentiation. It's the way the body decides, or differentiates, between different amino acid sequences to make different proteins for different tissues, whether they be hoof proteins or hair proteins or stomach proteins or whatever.

Here is where protein quality comes in. A poor quality protein is one for which all of the essential amino acids are not available in the right quantity or proportion to make body proteins. The term "essential amino acids" describes those that the horse cannot produce or that cannot be produced in adequate quantity to promote body protein synthesis. There are 9 amino acids that cannot be produced, and therefore must be in the diet. These are methionine, threonine, tryptophan, histidine, isoleucine, leucine, lysine, valine, and phenylalanine, with arginine, tyrosine and cysteine thought to be "semi-essential." Furthermore—and unfortunately—the horse does not have the ability to store amino acids, so any amino acids that don't get utilized end up being destroyed. But the story doesn't end there. The unused amino acids go the liver to be destroyed by splitting the molecule into two parts: an amino group and an organic acid.

The amino group quickly becomes ammonia, which is converted to urea. Urea enters the blood and is filtered out by the kidney to be excreted in the urine. This may put a burden on the liver and the kidneys of the older horse.

The organic acid can be used for energy, stored as fat, or converted to glucose. This has significant implications for the insulin resistant horse because when glucose is elevated, insulin rises—so a poor quality protein can actually cause insulin to rise. We think of sugar and starch doing that, but it could also happen with a poor quality protein, and this, too, can lead to laminitis. Furthermore, a poor quality protein can also make the horse use his own muscle tissue to make up the missing amino acids—and this may lead to muscle wasting. As you can see, then, there are lots of reasons to feed quality protein.

Animal protein sources are of the highest quality but horses are herbivorous. Therefore, quality protein can be created by feeding several plant sources, thereby having them complement one another with a mixture of amino acids. I offer some suggestions in my book, *Whole Foods and Alternative Feeds.*[5]

Fat digestion

Most of the fat in your horse's diet is in the form of triglycerides. These are large molecules that have a three-carbon "backbone" called glycerol, onto which three fatty acids are attached. The exact fatty acids vary according to the source and can be named by their chemical characteristics (i.e., omega system). But regardless of the type of fatty acids linked to glycerol, the triglyceride must be dismantled, or digested before it can be utilized.

Triglycerides are digested by enzymes called lipases, produced by the pancreas and the small intestine. Lipases split the fatty acids away from the glycerol molecule. They are later reassembled into triglycerides that are needed for the horse's cells. Because they are fatty and the blood is watery, triglycerides are packaged (along with cholesterol and phospholipids that are produced by the liver) into lipoproteins, where they can travel freely to the cells. This is a complex process that is beyond the scope of this book.

I do want to make the case for fats in the diet. Fat, as opposed to sugar and starch, is a really good source of energy for the horse. It has more than double the number of calories for every gram. If your horse needs extra calories, you can feed a fairly large amount—one cup (8 fluid ounces or 240 ml) per day for a horse at maintenance or lightly exercised; or up to two cups per day for the heavily exercised horse. If you do choose to feed that much fat, take about 4-6 weeks to build up to a large level because it takes about that much time for the body to adjust to digesting it.

Fat also has the benefit of slowing down the motility of the gastrointestinal tract, which then allows digestion of starch to be complete. This ends up having somewhat of a protective effect so that the starch doesn't reach the hindgut.

Vitamins and Minerals

Vitamins by themselves do not require digestion but are instead released during the digestion of more complex molecules. Water soluble vitamins—vitamin C and the eight B vitamins—are absorbed directly from the small intestine into the blood stream. Beta carotene from plants is converted to vitamin A inside the small intestine and is later packaged with the other fat soluble vitamins (vitamins D, E, and K) inside lipoproteins.

Minerals are absorbed directly into the bloodstream, about half of them here and the other half from the hindgut. Calcium, an exception, is absorbed in the early part of the small intestine but it needs vitamin D to be absorbed, so make sure your horse is getting plenty of sunlight; if he is not, make sure that he gets vitamin D in his diet. The good news about calcium is that the amount absorbed depends on the amount already in the horse's blood. If the horse has sufficient calcium, he will not absorb as much from his feed; if he needs more calcium, a larger amount will be absorbed.

Trace minerals (iron, zinc, copper, manganese, etc.) are normally chelated (attached) to amino acids inside the small intestine, facilitating their absorption. Their levels can influence each other's bioavailability (i.e., too much iron can interfere with zinc absorption), so it is important for minerals to be in balance in the entire diet.[6]

Hindgut

The hindgut encompasses the cecum, the large colon, the small colon, and the rectum; feedstuffs can remain here for 36 to 48 hours. The cecum and large colon are the major sites of microbial fermentation and absorption of fermentation products.

Cecum

The cecum is a fermentation vat very similar to a rumen but it has about 32 quarts in capacity compared to about 32 gallons the rumen holds, so it's about a fourth of the size. Nevertheless, it is pretty large and feed will stay in the cecum for about 7 hours. In the cecum, billions and billions of bacteria and protozoa produce enzymes that can digest fiber.

The design of the cecum seems a little crazy, frankly. The entrance to the cecum from the small intestine is at the top and so is the exit into the large colon. The entrance and exit are also quite close together. So picture this: You have all of this fiber that was not digested in the small intestine coming into the cecum where gravity pushes it to the bottom. The cecum is a very muscular organ that can contract and push on this forage and mix it with water and digestive fluids and all of the bacteria and enzymes, but in order for the muscles to push the forage mixture out through the top to get to the large colon, the cecum needs to be full; it has to have enough volume of materials so that when it contracts, it squishes the matter out through the top. It's like squishing a toothpaste tube on the bottom; it goes out through the top.

If the cecum is not full, then the process is hindered and the matter won't get conducted into the large colon for the next stage of digestion. This can lead to impaction colic.

Sand can also accumulate over time leading to sand colic. Horses will typically consume some dirt (or sand) while grazing outdoors, or will eat some bedding inside the stall. This foreign, undigestable material will stay on the bottom of the cecum, slowly building up until a full blown colic episode erupts. The only way to get it out of the cecum is for there to be enough forage to fill the organ sufficiently that material can be pushed out the top.

This is how you prevent colic—allow your horse to fill his cecum by grazing on forage, have water always available, and keep him moving to increase blood flow to the area.

Large colon

With the cecum full and able to do its job, it pushes the partially digested fiber into the large colon. What happens here? The large colon has about an 80 quart capacity; this is where billions and billions of resident bacteria continue to digest fiber. They digest (or ferment, more accurately) fiber into volatile fatty acids which the horse uses to provide calories—in fact, this is how your horse gets calories from hay.

Fiber

There are five different types of fiber I'd like you to be aware of. **Cellulose** is a water insoluble fiber, as is **hemicellulose.** Cellulose and hemicellulose are digestible by the bacteria. Another fiber, **lignin**, is not. Lignin is like wood; the more mature the grass is when it's cut to make hay, the more lignin it will contain.

If you look at your hay analysis report[7], it will show a number for neutral detergent fiber or NDF; this is a measurement of cellulose, hemicellulose, and lignin; this is the best measure of how digestible your hay is. If the number is high, over 60%, for example, the hay will not provide very many calories for your horse because it will contain a lot of lignin.

There are two other kinds of fiber: **pectin** and **mucilages**. These are water-soluble fibers that form a gel which actually helps push the fiber out of the cecum. Also, if the horse has ingested any dirt or sand–a concern for sand colic–you may give him psyllium (which is high in mucilages) which produces a gel that helps the sand move out of the cecum. Psyllium is often given for a week out of every month, but it can be fed more often, even daily, depending on the soil condition in your horse's environment.[8] A daily dose of psyllium has also been shown to lower blood insulin by inhibiting glucose absorption.

Hindgut bacteria

Let's talk about what the hindgut bacteria do. They ferment these fibers to three types of volatile fatty acids: acetate, butyrate, and propionate. These provide calories for your horse. Fermentation also results in the formation of heat, and water, and gas. Since the horse cannot normally release gas through the mouth (as cows can), the horse has adapted to produce less gas. However, the over-production of gases can occur when the horse is abruptly offered a large amount of a new feed.

These bacteria also can digest protein and produce their own amino acids, but unfortunately those amino acids are not absorbed out of the large colon and so they cannot benefit your horse.

More helpfully, these bacteria produce B vitamins, of which there are eight.[9] The hindgut bacteria also produce vitamin K.

The hindgut is a major component of your horse's immune function. You know the old saying "no hoof, no horse." I like to say "no bacterial flora, no horse," because these bacteria protect the immune function by preventing pathogens from entering the blood and the lymphatic system. The health of the hindgut is critical to your horse's overall immune function.

Small colon and rectum

The next portion of the hindgut is the small colon, which performs a very simple function: It absorbs water and forms fecal balls. Then this waste goes into the rectum, which is basically a holding chamber, until your horse defecates and releases the manure out of the anus.

Manure

Manure offers a good picture of your horse's overall health. It's a good idea to get accustomed to what your horse's manure looks like on a normal basis because changes can indicate health problems. If manure changes, for example, to a darker color, that could indicate the presence of blood. If it gets too hard and dry, that can indicate that your horse is not drinking enough water. If there's a lot of undigested feed, that says that your horse may not be producing sufficient digestive enzymes (common in older horses). So keep an eye on your horse's manure.

Chapter Two: Supporting Organs

Pancreas

The pancreas is a very complex organ that is heavily involved in digestion as well as in hormonal responses.

The pancreas produces sodium bicarbonate from cells called duct cells. The pancreas also performs the exocrine function, which means that it produces digestive enzymes. These are secreted by the acinar cells. And finally the pancreas has what's called an endocrine or hormonal function.

Within the pancreas, there are clusters (called eyelets) of three types of cells, which each have a different endocrine function; they are alpha, beta and delta.

The alpha cells produce glucagon, which is a hormone that does the opposite of insulin. Whereas insulin takes glucose out of the blood and puts it into the tissues, glucagon signals the liver to convert stored glycogen to glucose which is put back into the blood. Glucagon works homeostatically with insulin to keep the blood glucose levels normalized.

The beta cells are responsible for producing insulin in response to elevated blood glucose. If the cells are resistant to insulin (as is the case with equine metabolic syndrome or equine Cushing's disease) the pancreas will secrete more insulin in an attempt to get the glucose into the cells. This hyperinsulinemia (high blood insulin) is similar to the early stages of Type II diabetes in humans, in which glucose is also elevated (hyperglycemia); however, in equines with metabolic syndrome, glucose is not usually elevated since the insulin eventually does its job. If the beta cells were no longer working, insulin production would cease, leading to insulin-dependent (Type I) diabetes as we see in humans. This is rare in horses.

The delta cells produce a hormone called somatostatin, which controls other hormones throughout the body. Relative to digestion, somatostatin controls hormones such as gastrin, which is involved in acid secretion by the stomach, and secretin, which regulates the amount of sodium bicarbonate.

Liver

The liver is a very important organ and certainly vital to life. It is responsible for producing lipoproteins, which transport fat throughout the body. It's involved in glucose storage in the form of glycogen. It's involved in protein metabolism, breaking down excess amino acids. It's involved in storing fat-soluble vitamins and some of the B vitamins. Very importantly, it is a detoxifying organ that removes toxins from the blood stream.

But the liver has only one role in digestion: it produces bile. You produce bile, your dog produces bile, and most other animals do. But most animals have the ability to store bile in a gallbladder, which is nothing more than a storage vat that can contract and give a good squirt of bile into the first section of the small intestine (duodenum) when fat is present. The horse doesn't have a gallbladder.

It turns out that's okay. The horse's liver produces bile continually, and sort of drips like a leaky faucet into the duodenum. This is one reason the horse can get accustomed to ingesting more fat but he has to adjust gradually.

Bile is an emulsifier, meaning it brings together watery substances and fatty substances so that they can stay together. Fat doesn't mix on its own with water. Enzymes are watery and don't like fat. So how do we get the two together so that the fat can be digested? Enter bile, the emulsifier which has the ability to hold onto the two of them and keep them close together so that the fat can be digested.

Chapter Three: Extras to Help Digestion

Pre- and Probiotics

Most horses do not require pre- and/or probiotics. If the horse is grazing on pasture, he's consuming a large number of healthful microbes. If he has plenty of land to move around on and he's not under stress and he has at least one buddy and he's got lots to eat and he's happy, then his hindgut is probably in good shape.

But as he gets older, his hindgut can get compromised in terms of bacterial population. If he's stressed in any way, whether it be from stalling or traveling or the loss of a buddy or isolation or not being able to move out of a stall or not enough exercise or forage restriction (a major problem), any of these situations can cause the bacterial population to falter.

That's when you want to make sure that he is getting a good prebiotic which feeds the live bacteria in the hindgut. Prebiotics are made by bacteria fermenting a specific medium (generally made from carbohydrates). These fermentation products do not contain carbohydrates, but are produced from them. They are often concentrated in digestive enzymes.

Probiotics are live microbes and they're really most important to add when the horse is stressed a great deal, but also when the horse is receiving antibiotics which destroy the good bacteria as well as the bad.

One side note… horses are also not designed to digest lactose found in milk or milk products (such as yogurt). Once a foal is weaned, he stops producing the enzyme, lactase. Adult horses are lactose intolerant. Feeding yogurt as a probiotic will only lead to indigestion.

Adding yeast to the horse's diet has benefits because yeast actually increases the pH of the cecum which prevents cecal acidosis (caused by stress, or by acid flowing into the digestive tract, or by being fed grain that can also lower the pH). Yeast is also good for horses that are in training or working hard or if a horse is losing weight. Pregnant or lactating mares can also benefit from supplemental yeast. I recommend a product called Yeast Plus (HorseTech), available on my website. But many products contain yeast—look for brewer's yeast or *Saccharomyces cerevisiea* on the label.

When choosing a probiotic supplement, be sure the number of colony forming units (CFUs) is high enough. Some popular brands are terribly low, not providing enough microbes for you, let alone your horse! Look for a CFU count in the billions, which is denoted by 10^9 (the 9 represents the number of zeros following the number). Anything less is not sufficient to be helpful for your horse.

If your horse has diarrhea or is expelling fecal liquid, it could be due to dying bacteria, in which case replenishing them with a potent probiotic would be helpful. These digestive issues can also be caused by inflammation within the hindgut, causing water to flood the digestive tract. Change of diet can cause inflammation, therefore, when making changes, give the hindgut bacterial population time to make the adjustment and add a pro/prebiotic to assist with the transition. And be consistent by feeding the same thing each day. New items or treats can be added in small quantities but any significant portion size should be introduced slowly. Otherwise your horse can colic. I have seen this many times when a warm bran mash is given once a week as a "comfort" food; this approach can be very dangerous.

Deworming

I won't spend much time on the subject of deworming but want to emphasize the importance of testing your horse's manure for worms every two to three months. Horses living in the same environment may show very different levels of infestation—one won't have very many worms and another may. So test each horse individually and deworm appropriately.

Keep in mind, though, that your horse may be infested with larvae from small strongyles; this may not show up on a fecal test. Tapeworms also may not show up, though you will likely see segments in the manure. If your horse is infested with larvae, yet they do not show up in the fecal exam, he may show other signs: He could have weight loss, he could colic, he may not be thrifty looking, his hair coat may be dull, he may have some diarrhea, or he may just have a general malaise about him that you really cannot pinpoint. That's when a five-day double dose of fenbendazole may be appropriate; it's marketed under the name Power Pac. Moxidectin will also work for this but is not safe for all horses. I sometimes recommend a once-a-year dose of praziquantel for tapeworms. But don't take my recommendation without first discussing this with your veterinarian.

Chapter Four: More Reasons for Forage

Horses are trickle feeders, which means they are designed to eat forage all the time, 24 hours a day. Yes, they do nap—they'll take a 15-20 minute nap periodically throughout the day which will add up to two to four hours, depending on the horse, but they don't sleep for two hours consecutively, and they don't lie down at night for an eight-hour sleep. Mostly, horses eat. The previous chapters should have demonstrated the mechanics of why this is so, but read on for more of the dangers of preventing a horse from eating the way his body is set up to do.

We've seen that he needs hay to chew to release saliva and prevent ulcers. Chewing is so critical for the horse that if you feed a lot of concentrates and don't feed enough hay, the horse is likely to compensate by chewing on wood. He may even eat his own manure in an effort to produce saliva.

As we read earlier, an empty stomach can also lead to ulcers because of small intestinal reflux into the stomach. Normally, the duodenal contents stay put, but they have a tendency to re-enter the stomach through the pyloric sphincter when the stomach is empty, leading to pyloric and duodenal ulcerations.

Cribbing is generally done to produce saliva to alleviate the pain of an ulcer. Please do not put a cribbing collar on a horse. It does not remove the urge to crib and is tormenting. Cribbing can often be cured. It may take a couple of years to accomplish, but with the right feeding regimen, that allows sufficient chewing on forage, along with freedom to explore the outdoors and socialize, most horses will no longer crib. Horses need to be able to recover from a cribbing habit, and forage free choice all the time is the first step. There are some horses that appear to be hopeless. Cribbing can be inherited, or can start very early in life if the foal experiences the stress of early weaning. But even the worst cribbers can be helped to some extent—it may not completely stop, but can be reduced.

Your horse needs hay to keep the hindgut bacteria in good shape. He needs it to keep the pH balanced; if it gets too low, it leads to cecal acidosis which can destroy the bacteria in the hindgut; this in turn can lead to leaky gut syndrome which causes the toxins from the dying bacteria to enter the bloodstream and that can lead to laminitis. Cecal acidosis can also lead to colic.

But here's another reason the horse is designed to eat all the time: the entire gastrointestinal tract is made of muscles that need to exercise and the only way they can do that is to move. They need to have something to move upon and that's what forage does. Forage flowing through the digestive tract all the time allows the digestive tract muscles to work; flabby muscles can twist or torque, or they can intussuscept (telescope)—increasing the risk of colic.

Hay restriction is incredibly stressful; it leads to the formation of stress hormones, in particular cortisol which raises insulin and insulin causes laminitis. Insulin also tells the body to hold onto fat because the horse sees himself as being in starvation mode. The horse perceives that as an emergency, a call to hold onto whatever body fat he has. In fact, if you're trying to get your horse to lose weight, restricting forage is the worst thing you can do, because if you restrict it enough, he'll lose weight (mainly as muscle), but his metabolic rate will slow down so dramatically that he'll easily gain weight on fewer calories than he used to have to maintain his weight. The elevated insulin will also put him at risk for laminitis. I've seen many relapses of laminitis when a well-intentioned horse owner puts the horse in a dry lot with very little hay; the horse becomes stressed, the insulin level goes way up, and we have a renewed case of laminitis.

The elevated cortisol response from stress also suppresses the immune function, making your horse more susceptible to infections and allergies, more susceptible toward developing EHV when traveling, and other illnesses including respiratory ailments, fungal infections, and negative reactions to vaccinations. As you can see, a whole slew of problems can occur when a horse's immune system is compromised.

Finally, without a steady flow of forage, the digestive tract simply does not function properly. You know how you want to hear those important gut sounds—they tell you that the digestive tract is in motion. Please read Appendix A on how to use your stethoscope to listen to gut sounds.

Forage keeps the digestive tract moving. A horse who spends his time standing in a stall, not able to walk around and not eating is a case of colic waiting to happen.

Chapter Five: Forage Free Choice

By now you understand the critical importance of allowing the horse to eat continuously. Here's how to do that in four basic steps.

Step number one—start with grass hay

Start with any grass hay—Bermuda, orchard grass, brome, timothy, Teff, to name a few. Avoid oat hay, crested wheat grass, rye grass; these are grain hays and they can be higher in starch. Alfalfa is great for boosting protein quality and is a good buffer for horses that are prone toward ulcers, but you don't want to feed it free choice. You want to add it sort of as a dessert or a condiment on the side. And never feed more than 50% of the hay ration as alfalfa because it can lead to intestinal stones.

Some horses are sensitive to alfalfa but it does not have to do with the protein content. It may more likely be due to the phytoestrogen levels (though this has not been proven) which can affect behavior or may—and that's a strong, "may"—lead to laminitis in some, but not many, horses.

Feeding forage free choice depends on using hay that is safe—that is low enough in starch and sugars and fructans for the horse to eat without limitation. How do you know if it is? That's step number two.

Two: Get your hay analyzed

Send in a sample of your hay to a reputable lab that analyzes hay for horses. You are looking for a report that gives you numbers applicable to horses, not cattle. Equi-Analytical is a laboratory that does that. You can connect with them online at www.equi-analytical.com. Order their Equi-tech test, which is a really good one (it provides information on carbohydrates as well as minerals) and reasonably priced. It is a wise investment that will help you understand the nutritional values of your hay.[10]

You are looking for two things, NSC and digestible energy.

NSC (non-structural carbohydrates) should be less than 12% on an as-fed or an as-sampled basis, not dry matter basis, because as-fed or as-sampled is what the horse is actually eating.

To calculate NSC, you add the WSC (water-soluble carbohydrates, representing simple sugars plus fructans) to the number for starch; if those two numbers total 12% or less, the hay is safe to feed free choice. This number includes fructans which do not significantly influence insulin levels. However, laminitis can occur from excessive bacterial fermentation of fructans reaching the hindgut, so it is important to limit the fructan levels (which can be approximated by taking the difference between WSC and ESC).

Sometimes the ESC plus starch number is useful. ESC (ethanol soluble carbohydrates) represents simple sugars. Since simple sugars contribute to hormonally influenced (elevated insulin) laminitis, you want the ESC plus starch to be less than 10%.

Digestible energy (again, on an as-sampled basis) is the number of megacalories per pound (or megacalories per kilogram for my international friends). It should be less than 0.88 Mcals/lb, or if you multiply that by 2.2, that will be 1.94 Mcals/kg. This is the highest caloric level you want your hay to provide.

If the hay is low in calories and it's low in sugar and starch, you can feed it free choice. This is logical.

If you want to maintain a healthy weight, you know you can eat all of the cucumbers and lettuce you want. Why? Because they're low in calories; conversely, you certainly know you cannot eat all the high-calorie, high-sugar chocolate chip cookies you want. If you stay with food that's low in calories and low in refined sugar and starch (even if you eat all that you want) then you're more likely to maintain a good, low weight, or even lose. The same thing is basically true for your horse, whether he is of normal weight or needs to lose weight. If he eats a diet that is based on low calorie hay and is low in sugar and starch, he is more likely to maintain or achieve a healthy weight. Now we come to step number three.

Three: Give your horse appropriate food and let him have all that he wants.

That's right. All that he wants. 24/7. Do not let him run out of hay, not even for ten minutes. He needs to trust that hay will always be available.

For this to work, a horse truly needs to have enough hay to last all day and to last all night. How do you know if he has enough? There has to be some hay left over when you go out to feed again. Let me say that again—*there has to be some hay left over*. If there is none left, it won't matter if he finished it a half hour earlier or if the supply ran out at two in the morning (and he's been standing there in pain and uncomfortable for several hours). Just the sight of that empty feeder or clear ground will be urging his instincts—and hormones—to direct his body into starvation protection mode. So make sure he never runs out. (Please refer to Appendix B for a personal letter you may want to share with others about bringing back the horse's instincts.)

When he realizes that he has all the hay that he wants, that he can walk away from it, take a nap, read the paper, talk to a friend and come back and find the hay is still there and he's not competing with other horses for it, then something miraculous happens. He starts to calm down. He starts to eat less. His hormonal levels start to normalize; he starts to lose weight if he's overweight, and oddly enough he starts to gain weight if he's underweight. He becomes a different horse.

So, yes, forage free choice 24/7. What you're looking for is that magic moment when he walks away from the hay. That's when he has said to you, "Ah, I got the message. I can go away and the hay will still be there when I get back."

Step four is patience

This process usually takes about three or four days, although for some it will take longer. At first your horse will overeat, but then he's going to self -regulate and start to eat less. It will happen. Allow his instincts to return that tell him he's satisfied; they may seem lost, but they can resurface.

A horse's behavior changes for the better when you start to feed forage free choice. It's remarkable to see: Whereas he used to grab at the hay at feeding time, now he kind of gives you a look to say *just go ahead and put it in the corner and I'll get to it later when I'm ready.* Horses fed forage free choice relax. They calm down. They become easier to train. They become less skittish and less sensitive. And every cell in the horse's body benefits because the immune system becomes stronger.

Occasionally you get a horse that just holds on and eats and eats and eats. One of my client's had a horse that took about three weeks to self-regulate; he just continued to eat and eat (actually gaining a little weight), which was difficult for the client to watch happening, but then all of a sudden the horse did the magical thing and walked away. That's when it started to all come into place. The horse started to eat less and lose weight.

Sometimes you will encounter a barn manager who doesn't want to feed forage free choice because of the supposed cost. The truth is that horses allowed to eat free choice and to self regulate actually eat less than they eat when they're starving or perceive themselves to be starving—those horses will inhale all available feed and beg for more.

Let the horse tell you how much he needs to eat. You may have heard that you should feed 1.5-2% (sometimes 3%) of the horse's weight as forage— where do you think we get those numbers? We get them by giving the horse all the hay that he wants and then measuring how much he eats; lo and behold, it's between 1.5-3% depending on his activity level and depending on his breed and so on.

So, those are the four steps: start with a grass hay, have it analyzed, don't ever let him run out not even for a few minutes, and then be patient.

Some cautionary advice about "helping" devices

If you are concerned about your horse eating too fast, you can use a slow feeder. Slow feeders are nice in helping your horse eat less, but let me caution you. You must give the horse time to get acclimated to the device. If you just put a slow feeder out (and preferably you want to use several) then it will cause frustration which is a form of stress, and what does stress do? It causes insulin to rise which tells his body to hold onto fat so you're defeating your purpose.

Keep slow feeders close to the ground to simulate a natural grazing stance. Feeders placed high can strain your horse's neck muscles as well as increase the chances of choke.

Once your horse accepts a slow feeder, put several in as many places as you can, encouraging your horse to investigate a new hay supply, and most importantly, encouraging your horse to move.

Grazing muzzles create the same challenge with stress. If it frustrates the horse, a grazing muzzle can defeat your purpose. Certainly you don't want to put a grazing muzzle on for more than two or three hours because your horse needs to have forage flowing through his system and restricting feed runs counter to that.

Exercise

Finally: the horse needs to move. Movement, movement, movement. I can't say it enough. Exercise is critical to digestive health–in truth, it is essential. The horse needs to move because when a horse moves his circulation improves, and circulation then feeds the muscles, which allows them to be in good tone and process nutrients. Exercise keeps the organs fit, too, allowing the forage to travel better through the digestive tract. A digestive tract in a body that is not moving is prone to colic; horses that are allowed to be turned out in as big an area as possible are the healthiest. So, if your horse is stalled, make sure he's got forage in his stall constantly but also give him every opportunity to leave the stall and move!

Questions and Answers

Getty Challenge.[11] Karen comments taking the Getty Challenge which calls for feeding forage free choice for 30 days and seeing the results. Karen has read disagreements from various people; she says, "They claim that horses don't really eat 24 hours a day." But she defends the practice, saying, "Of course they don't, but having the hay available is what matters for their physical and emotional well-being. Some folks don't yet understand that having the hay available is a true stress-reducing strategy."

Answer: Exactly, Karen. They don't constantly eat because they know they can come back to it when they need it. Thank you for spreading this message to other horse owners.

Insufficient hay available. Karen asks what horse owners can do if they're not able to get enough hay.

Answer: Last year, there was a terrible drought in many areas around the country. Here in Ohio, the drought made it difficult to find hay. Using Craig's List, I found hay in several places; I actually tested all of it. (I got a reputation around here as the crazy lady with the baggies because I was testing all the hay until I found the batch that I liked.) The website www.hayexchange.com has hay available as well.

If you still cannot find hay, you can feed hay cubes free choice. You do need to break them up into small pieces so it's labor intensive; it helps to add a little water to soften them somewhat; they don't get really soft. There is bagged hay, too. Chopped forage is an option; however, it generally contains molasses so if your horse is insulin resistant, that would not be an option.

Triple Crown has something called Safe Starch which is full-length hay, not chopped. It does have vitamins and minerals added so you would not necessarily need to add a vitamin/mineral supplement if you fed enough of it, usually around 20 pounds, but if you feed less then you can add a vitamin/mineral supplement.

Pony with chronic laminitis, pancreas and liver involvement. Sonja has a 33-year-old pony that is chronically laminitic. Her osteopath said that the pony's pancreas isn't working properly and that the pancreas needs nutritional support. During the pony's recent laminitis episode, the osteopath, who practices Chinese medicine, said that the organ most affected was the liver and a horse with a stressed pancreas will have a stressed liver to compensate for the pancreas. Sonja asks if this could be true, and if there is anything she could feed to support the pony. She also asks for any information about metabolic syndrome, Cushing's, or laminitis.

Answer: Parts of Sonja's question bring up various disorders for which I'll refer you to my topical books, which go into helpful detail about management of these disorders, e.g. laminitis, Cushing's disease.

Let me start to answer Sonja's question with an important reminder: Ponies are a little different from horses. Ponies really don't need as much protein and they cannot tolerate as much fat, sugar and starch as horses can. But just like horses, ponies, minis, donkeys, mules, and hinnies should be fed forage free choice. Never restrict forage because ponies, donkeys and related species are more susceptible to burning a lot of body fat to make up for missing calories, and this can lead to a very dangerous and deadly disorder known as hyperlipemia.

Antioxidants can help the pancreas. However, I'm not sure how the osteopath decided that the pancreas wasn't working. I don't know if your pony is insulin resistant but that is not a problem with the pancreas. The pancreas is not problematic with insulin resistance; the cells are resistant to insulin. At the cellular level, insulin is not able to adequately do its job of removing glucose from the blood and allowing it to enter the cells. Consequently, the pancreas continues to pump out more insulin in hopes that it will eventually lower blood glucose. So insulin remains elevated. It is important to not cause an even higher rise in insulin; therefore, avoiding feeds high in sugar and starch are critical for the insulin resistant animal.

As for the liver "compensating," frankly, I do not see a connection. The liver and pancreas are two very different organs—the pancreas produces enzymes and hormones that the liver does not produce. One does not compensate for the other. Sonja mentions giving herbs such as milk thistle and dandelion root to help cleanse the liver, but neither of these are really doing anything to prevent laminitis. Cleansing the liver will help detoxify it if, for example, there's any type of liver damage or immune system problem or allergies, but it won't make a difference to the amount of insulin the pancreas is pumping out that's leading to laminitis. So, you need to pay attention to the insulin level and not worry so much about the pancreas except to keep the horse healthy in general by providing enough antioxidants.

Malabsorption syndrome. Cristine has a horse that has been losing weight and appears to have an immune system problem. The lab work shows that he's not absorbing much; she doesn't know what specific test was run. She has fed several different probiotics and he's still losing weight.

Answer: Malabsorption Syndrome is a very serious disorder in which the digestive system fails to extract nutrients from food. There are various carbohydrate absorption tests available to detect problems within the small intestine. If the pancreas is involved, there is likely a deficiency in enzyme production, which is not directly treatable. However, oral digestive enzymes may help somewhat.

One of the main causes of malabsorption in humans is gluten intolerance, and gluten intolerance does exist in horses. So look at the grains and hay you are feeding to eliminate any source of gluten. Wheat, rye and barley all contain gluten, regardless of the form in which you feed them, even in something like rye grass. Oats do not contain gluten in themselves; however, if oats are processed in a plant that also processes gluten-carrying grains (and most oats are), they may pick up trace amounts of gluten. Rice bran does not contain gluten. Corn does not either—but don't ever feed corn to horses; it's very poorly digested and therefore increases the risk of laminitis.

Also, if the pancreas is involved, I would feed high levels of antioxidants. There is a supplement called Su-Per Anti-Oxidant (Gateway) which you may want to switch to, and then add some flaxseed meal for omega-3s. Su-Per Anti-Oxidant is available on my website store.

I would certainly have a complete blood workup done on him. Test for fibrinogen levels, which measures inflammation, and do a serum chemistry panel to test for normal liver and kidney function.

Nephrosplenic entrapment leading to frequent colic. Susan has a horse that has frequent bouts of colic and has a lot of gas. He lies down and stretches and he appears to have some type of impaction. He'll go for a while without passing any manure. He is on pasture 24/7. Susan's veterinarian feels that the horse most likely has adhesions because he had a nephrosplenic entrapment (in which the large colon becomes hooked over the nephrosplenic ligament) and therefore he cannot handle the bulk from hay or alfalfa hay. So in addition to grass, he gets alfalfa pellets that are soaked and beet pulp and some senior grain. He's also getting rice bran oil, Flaxin 3 (flaxseed meal by Med-Vet Pharmaceuticals). He gets aloe vera juice, salt, and he gets a probiotic called Forco (Forco Colorado). He drinks water well most of the time, and a small amount of added apple juice encourages him to drink during cold weather. Susan is wondering what else she can do.

Answer: First, because Flaxin 3 has only added minerals, not vitamins, I would switch to something that contains both vitamins and minerals and has a large amount of vitamin E that's ground flaxseed based; PreOx (HorseTech) at a double dose (2 scoops per day) would replace the Flaxin 3. You can find that on my website. The increased vitamin E (5000 IU at a double dose) in PreOx can actually help with the adhesions. Of course, the longer it's been since he had the entrapment, the less likely it is to help with adhesions, but it can still help some. Make sure that the senior feed has no starch or molasses in it; in fact, you know you could probably eliminate the senior feed altogether because he'll be getting the vitamins and minerals he needs from the PreOx, and if he needs more calories you could add some beet pulp and alfalfa pellets. If you think that he has ulcers, I know you're giving aloe vera juice and a probiotic, and you might also give some Starting Gate Granules (SBS Equine), with lecithin and apple pectin, which will help alleviate ulcers, or you can give just plain lecithin at about half a cup a day.

Wild horse digestion. Siobhan is curious about the digestion process of the wild horse, how it would be affected by the diversity of his diet. Compared to a domesticated horse whose diet needs to be changed gradually, how does a feral horse's digestion work, when his diet is changing all the time and there are different foods available to him?

Answer: That's a very, very good question. It mainly has to do with the fact that horses in a wild setting are not eating significant amounts of grains and they're not eating large amounts of sugars and starches. In the domesticated situation, we tend to feed commercially fortified feeds high in sugars and starches (e.g. cereal grains, sweet feeds), changes in which are very difficult for the horse's body to adjust to. The bacterial flora has to adjust and the amylase has to increase. Some adjustment can happen quickly, but generally not quickly enough; in truth the horse really needs several weeks to get adjusted to a change in cereal grain diet.

Furthermore, horses in a wild setting do not eat the same grasses every day; they are consuming natural, varied forages that are not fertilized and are allowed to grow wild. Compare that to the domesticated horse dining on lush, "improved" (fertilized, mono-culture) pastures, which tend to be higher in sugar and starch.

And a final major difference is that the feral horse is exercised simply by the demands of his environment, which keeps the metabolic rate healthier. They don't get overweight and they eat little bits here and there.

I often like to add variety to horses' feeds rather than give them the same thing day in and day out. In my teleseminar and book on Whole Foods, I talk about adding different foods to a horse's diet to improve their diet's overall nutrition makeup. But you can't feed large amounts of these things without doing it consistently. Of course, you can give a horse a few strawberries every now and then and it's not going to make a big difference, but if you intend to feed a whole quart of strawberries, then you had better work up to that gradually because the bacterial flora are going to need time to adjust. The horse in a wild situation has variety in small amounts. Variety in small amounts is beneficial; variety in large amounts takes time for the bacteria to adjust.

Feeding horse with poor teeth. Becky has an older cushingoid, insulin-resistant horse that is struggling now with being colicky. His teeth are wearing out so he can't eat hay very well. He gets fed four times a day and he doesn't get much grass because of the risk of laminitis.

Answer: This is a topic handled in more detail in my Cushing's or laminitis books, but, briefly, you still want to feed forage free choice, and since he can't chew hay very well, you may have to use hay cubes or a chopped hay. You could conceivably take a chopped hay and soak it and drain the water off to remove the added sugar, a rather expensive option. But hay cubes softened in water will work fairly well.

You mentioned that he can't graze on grass because of laminitis issues. You might be able to allow him to graze if you pay attention to the ambient temperature and also test your pasture. Here is why: Grass tends to be higher in sugar and starch in the spring and fall when the nighttime temperatures are cold but followed by warm, sunny days. Once the nighttime temperatures stay above 40 degrees for most of the night, then the grass will relinquish its sugars and starches during the night; at that point, the safest time to allow grazing would be early in the morning before the sun gets too high. Around 10 or 10:30 in the morning then you can pull the horse off the pasture and put him in a dry lot with hay, or softened hay cubes, free choice. Certainly toward the end of the summer, towards July into August, and again after a hard freeze when the grass goes dormant, test your pasture, because you may be pleasantly surprised to see that the sugar and starch levels and fructan levels are really quite low, making the pasture a safe option for continual grazing.

Water from the small colon. Chris has a 13-year-old gelding whose manure is normal in itself, but when he defecates, he first expels liquid, then manure, followed by more liquid. It's a considerable amount and quite messy. The horse has hay 24/7. Chris has tried the following, none of which worked: colloidal silver; deworming for encysted parasites; Life Force supplement; a probiotic called Daily Start. What should she do?

Answer: The small colon is designed to absorb water so that the manure can dry out. So something is preventing that from happening. The likely cause would be inflammation in the small colon. I would suggest a couple of things to reduce inflammation. First, add vitamin B1. I have found that thiamine or vitamin B1 in high dosages (3,000 mg/day) helps with this type of situation. This is not scientifically determined; it's strictly anecdotal from working with clients whose horses have had similar problems. I offer a custom, concentrated vitamin B1 product that HorseTech made for me for another client's horse with a similar problem. Give 3,000 mg/day for about a month and you should start to see some improvement.

The other thing that you can do to reduce inflammation is to give a curcumin preparation; curcumin is a powerful anti-inflammatory. Cur-Ost (Nouvelle Research) offers several preparations that are made with curcumin and Boswellia (another anti-inflammatory). These are very potent. You could start out with Cur-Ost EQ Green and move up perhaps to their Plus Formula. These are also available through my website store.

You can also simply purchase the spice turmeric (which contains curcumin). You might be able to buy it in bulk at Whole Foods or online.

Certainly you want to make sure that you're feeding enough antioxidants. Good preparations for this are Su-Per Anti-Oxidant (Gateway), Glänzen Complete (HorseTech), or PreOx (HorseTech), all available through my website. Glänzen Complete and PreOx are ground flaxseed based which means they contain omega 3s. Su-Per Anti-Oxidant is not; you'd have to add some flaxseed meal or some chia seeds to add omega 3s. The goal is to be anti-inflammatory. Certainly give no products with soybean or corn oil, both of which promote inflammation.

Look also at any changes in the diet—a new hay or weeds in the pasture. Help the hindgut bacteria by offering a prebiotic called Ration Plus (S.E. Monroe), which contains large amounts of fermentation products. I have seen positive results with this, as well.

Feeding hay before grain. Susan has heard that you should feed hay before you feed any grain or pelleted feed, because it is better for the horse to have some hay going through the digestive process first. Is that true?

Answer: Yes, it is true. If you feed grain without any hay, grain leaves the stomach and enters the small intestine very quickly, potentially reaching the hindgut undigested —and that increases the risk of laminitis. With hay present, the whole digestive process is slowed because hay takes more time for the horse to ingest and process. Furthermore, the presence of fiber slows down the absorption of glucose (from starch digestion) thereby creating a more even rise in blood insulin levels.

Shetland pony eating more than Tennessee walkers. Christine has a little Shetland pony that was obese when she got him a year ago. She is a "huge dedicated believer in free choice" but she says she could give more and more and more and more, and still it's rare to find any leftover in the morning. He's eating more hay than the big horses, than the two Tennessee walkers. She uses a hay net with very small holes; that often has hay still in it in the morning, but the pony is not losing weight.

Answer: The success of feeding forage free choice depends on its consistency. Of course, you MUST make sure you've tested the hay so that it is low enough in sugar and starch to be appropriate to feed free choice. Then pay close attention to whether there is, in fact, hay left in the morning. If there are times when there is none, that means he has, in fact, run out and so in his mind, he's still thinking he is going to run out. He never gets the message consistently that it's always going to be there. I know this is really hard to do, but what I'm suggesting is that you give him more so that he could never run out, ever.

Christine responds: I mean hay is there in the morning five nights out of seven, but you're right; some nights he's eaten it all so that's enough for him to have not gotten the message metabolically, correct?

Dr. Getty: If he runs out of hay and he's stressed and looking for more—looking for every last nibble—then he will continue to perceive that he is not going to have all that he wants. With this perception governing his instinctual drive to avoid starvation, he cannot self regulate.

And encourage movement. It's so important, I will say it again: *Encourage movement.* Put hay nets in various places so that he can walk around to get to them.

In conclusion, I hope you've come away with a good understanding of the horse's digestive tract anatomy, along with a grasp of the way nutrients are handled and the reasons some nutrients are more important than others to the horse's digestive health. I hope all of this information has also prepared you not only to commit to feeding appropriate forage free choice, but also to defend the practice against those who would try to convince you otherwise.

Educating yourself as a horse owner in the science that grounds best feeding practices is vitally important to ensuring the optimal health of your horse—that animal who works for you, plays with you, and gives you such abiding trust and affection.

Your horse looks to you to honor the way he is made, and feed him accordingly. You owe that to him, just as you owe it to yourself to know you have done your very best for him.

Appendix A: Learn to Use A Stethoscope... Before You Need It

Your emergency kit likely includes a stethoscope—a highly valuable piece of equipment during any urgent health situation. Knowing your horse's normal heart rate and gut sounds beforehand will allow you to better assess the seriousness of the situation—so use your stethoscope now.

A resting pulse is typically between 32 and 40 beats per minute (ponies' are slightly higher). Place the stethoscope in front of the girth area, just behind the elbow. Using the sweep second hand on your watch or a stop watch (usually a feature on your cell phone), count the number of beats for 30 seconds and double it to get beats per minute. Measure at various times of day, before and after eating, and at any change in circumstances or activity level; this will give you a clear idea of how your horse generally responds to his environment. Marked deviation from normal (without obvious explanation such as exercise) can indicate the presence of infection, pain, or illness.

Your stethoscope is especially useful for listening to gut sounds. It is normal and healthy for sounds to come from the digestive tract due to the movement of feed, gas, and fluid. Intestines are made of muscles; processing forage continuously provides the necessary exercise to keep these muscles in good condition. Normally, the sounds will be low in pitch with some growling. Colic occurs when there is a change within the intestines, ordinarily due to obstruction, gas, or torsion, and sounds change or stop altogether. If you don't hear any noise, or if the sounds have become higher pitched, significantly slowed, or sound hollow, it likely indicates colic and you should contact your vet immediately.

Practice listening to four areas of the gut: along the upper barrel and the lower flank area on both sides. Generally speaking, sounds from the upper left come from the small colon and tend to be high pitched and of short duration. The lower left has sounds from the large colon. On the upper right, the sounds come from the large colon and cecum whereas the lower right has the large colon. However, the point of origin for gut sounds is not completely predictable; the important thing is to identify a variation from your horse's normal sounds.

Deviations from normal in pulse or gut sounds may have many possible explanations, so unless you have extensive experience, you should never put yourself in the position of diagnosing colic or other disorders. But you can be a valuable resource to your veterinarian if you know what is normal for your horse and can identify a change, before illness happens.

Appendix B: Bring Back the Horse's Instincts

Dear Horseperson,

I write this letter in hopes that you will take what it says to heart and share it with others.

The issue is free choice forage feeding.

I respect and honor the way horses are made – they are different – unique, really. In a suitable, native environment, they are quite capable of taking care of themselves. They are free to eat and roam and, well, be horses. Domestication involves removing them from their natural setting, but that doesn't change who they are. Horses have physiological and mental needs and those needs are being ignored.

I have very deep convictions on allowing a horse's instincts to take hold. Many horses have lost their ability to express them, but they can resurface. Last month, I wrote about the stress of forage restriction. Some have said that what I am describing appears to be a road to increased obesity and an increased risk of laminitis. But they are grossly mistaken.

When we see images of wild horses running free, we all experience the hush, the chill, and the awe of their power and majesty. That is Nature at her best – allowing these incredible animals to live as they are intended. Why is it that we don't see our own domesticated horses in the same way? Why is it that we think we can confine them to a small area for hours at a time, give them a few "square meals" each day and expect them to be right, physically and mentally? Are they not the same horses that long ago lived a different life?

It's been said that our horses have become different – that horses living in the wild don't suffer from the ravages of insulin resistance, the main cause of laminitis. Yes, it's true -- we don't see laminitis when horses are free to feed themselves. But we do see insulin resistance, and that's a blessing.

Insulin resistance is the body's way of avoiding starvation. During a harsh winter, when the food supply is sparse, horses will hold on to body fat to help them survive. They do this by having an elevated blood insulin level. When insulin is high, the cells cannot release fat. This is a survival mechanism.

We duplicate this when we restrict forage. The horse responds the same way—he is in survival mode! And he holds on to body fat.

Anything that causes insulin to rise will keep a horse fat. Hundreds of studies with humans confirm the connection between elevated insulin and obesity. Stress causes obesity in humans. Why? Because cortisol (the stress hormone) causes insulin to rise. At the cellular level, the same is true for horses. We have equine studies to show how insulin rises during stress. So why isn't this being extrapolated to obesity in horses?

Perhaps it's because it doesn't seem to make sense that eating more causes weight loss. But we know that humans best lose weight by eating small meals throughout the day – grazing, if you will. And we also know that starving oneself will result in weight loss (mostly muscle loss) but will slow down the metabolic rate so dramatically, that the weight comes back on with far fewer calories than it originally took to maintain one's weight. Yet the studies we choose to do using horses involve starving the horse to get him to lose weight. Which he does. And we celebrate. The conventional advice appears to work: Give the horse hay equal to 1.5% of his body weight, keep him in a stall much of the day so he cannot graze, and he loses weight! And if he doesn't, reduce the amount of hay to 1%! The idiom, "not seeing the forest for the trees," comes to mind. What is the big picture? What are you left with? A horse with less muscle mass, stressed to the max, with a sluggish metabolism so he will never live a normal life of grazing on pasture again. Never.

We have forced our horses to abandon their instincts.

They no longer get the inner signal that tells them to stop eating. To help you appreciate this, I'd like you to think about your childhood. When you were a toddler, you ate what you needed, and when you were no longer hungry, you stopped eating. Yes, you were coddled to finish your green beans, or no dessert! So you ate more to get that reward. But your instincts (yes, you had them back then) were to eat only what your body required. As you grew, you discovered that eating has more rewards than just getting dessert; eating is comforting, it cures stress, boredom, or disappointment, and is just plain fun! You likely don't eat only when you're hungry; you eat whenever you gather with friends or celebrate a special occasion. And guess what? Now that you're grown, those instincts to eat only what your body needs have long faded.

Horses are a different story. They do not succumb to the pressures of society to influence their appetites. But when they are forced to eat on our schedules, they quickly become out of touch with that innate ability to eat slowly, a little at a time, and stop when satisfied. Instead, they eat quickly, ravenously, with barely a breath in between each bite, because they do not know when their next meal will be available. When it gets close to feeding time they pace, bob their heads, paw the ground, and make strange noises. This is not normal; it is a result of what we have done to our horses. We, well-meaning horse owners and caregivers, are putting our horses into survival mode!

Horses are unlike humans in one very significant way.

Their digestive tract is not the same as ours. The biology that drives the horse's digestion is indisputable: The horse's stomach produces acid continuously, necessitating the action of chewing to release acid-neutralizing saliva. The digestive tract is made of muscles and needs to be exercised to prevent colic by having a steady flow of forage running through it. The cecum (the hindgut where forage is digested by billions of microbes) has both its entrance and exit at the top, thereby requiring it to be full so material can exit, lest it become impacted.

I appeal to you to look at this logically.

You should not put your horse in a dry lot or a stall with no hay. You should test your hay, make sure it is suitable for the horse (low in sugar, starch, and calories) and put it in lots of slow feeders, placed everywhere you can – encouraging your horse to move! Exercise, even a small amount will make a difference. A larger amount will make a bigger difference.

When a horse loses weight the right way, his metabolic rate stays sound and he will be able to graze on pasture again. Perhaps you will have to limit it a bit, but maybe not. Some supplements may be helpful. I have seen hundreds of cases over the years where horses have returned to a normal life – healthy, full of vigor, with no grass restrictions.

Let your horse tell you how much he needs to eat.

Show him that he can start trusting his instincts—that's the strong message you want him to understand. And you do that by being invariably trustworthy about feeding. Start by giving him more hay (that you've tested for suitability) than he could possibly eat – enough to last all day and enough so there is some left over in the morning. That means he needs to always have forage available. If he runs out, he will never get the message and will continue to overeat and continue to be fat.

Let me repeat that… If he runs out, even for 10 minutes, he will never get the message and will continue to overeat and continue to be fat. And worse, the hormonal response to this stress can induce a laminitis attack or relapse. I've seen this more times than I can count.

It may take a few weeks (though most of the time it is far shorter than that) for the magic moment to occur – when he walks away from the hay, knowing that it will still be there when he wants it. And then, watch his instincts start to return… just like yours were when you were a small child… where he will eat only what his body needs to be healthy. (You'll notice a beautiful change in his behavior, too.)

I have many, many clients who have put their trust in me and done this for their horses with success. It is not easy to do at first—I understand. But when done properly, it works—the overweight horse loses weight. The horse with chronic laminitis doesn't suffer any more. The horse with Cushing's disease can live a longer, healthier life. Equine metabolic syndrome becomes a thing of the past. And the owners… ah, the owners… can throw away all that worry and experience the sheer joy horse ownership brings.

I know that I am a trailblazer.

This seems like something new. Actually, if you think about it, it is so old, that it *is* new! But that's how change happens. We used to feed oats to horses – gallons of oats every day. We now know that a large amount of starch is detrimental. I am encouraged by this change, not only because of its own value, but because it tells me that there is every likelihood that feeding forage free choice will also come to be accepted as mainstream.

I am doing everything I possibly can to help horse owners and professionals understand this basic, foundational concept. I have 7 years of postgraduate study in the field of animal nutrition. I work completely independently of feed, supplement, and pharmaceutical companies. My approach is based on observation and years of excellent results. There is no better science than that.

For the growing community of horse owners and managers who allow their horses free choice feeding, I have set up a special forum for you to share your experiences with each other and to let me and others know how you're doing. It is a place for support, celebrations, congratulations, and idea sharing. Go to jmgetty.blogspot.com.

Most sincerely,

Dr. Juliet M. Getty

Please share this article with your fellow horsemen and women. Permission to reprint commercially is granted if prior written notice is given to Dr. Getty at gettyequinenutrition@gmail.com. No editorial changes may be made without her approval.

Notes

Introduction

[1] Miniature horses, ponies, donkeys, and mules have the same digestive tract anatomy has full sized horses. Donkeys and mules, however, have more efficient microbial digestion of forage in the hindgut than horses. Therefore, they are better able to digest fiber, resulting in less consumption than horses when presented with free choice hay. This natural adaptation is favorable for donkeys because they do not need as many calories as a horse to maintain a normal body weight. When offered starchy concentrates (cereal grains), they will generally moderate their intake, but don't risk giving them starchy or sweet feed because they are prone toward developing insulin resistance, and hence laminitis (founder). Miniature horses and ponies are also genetically predisposed toward insulin resistance.

Chapter One

[2] The horse's ability to produce saliva declines as he ages, which makes it especially important to watch for problems such as choke in the aging horse.

[3] Do not ever feed corn. Corn is not well digested and can be risky to feed to horses, so save it for your chickens.

[4] Each book in the *Spotlight on Equine Nutrition Series* covers the nutritional aspects of a specific topic in equine health. These books are available at www.GettyEquineNutrition.com and through Amazon; they are also available in Kindle format.

[5] Part of the *Spotlight on Equine Nutrition* book series. See above.

[6] I offer customized mineral balancing services. Contact me through www.GettyEquineNutrition.com.

[7] On your hay analysis report, these is also a number for acid detergent fiber or ADF; that's just cellulose and lignin without the hemicellulose, and it's not as useful a number as neutral detergent fiber (NDF).

[8] Moreaux, S.J.J., Nichols, J.L., Bowman, J,G.P., and Hatfield, P.G. 2011. Psyllium lowers blood glucose and insulin concentrations in horses. *Journal of Equine Veterinary Science,* 31, 160-165.

[9] Four out of the eight B vitamins (thiamine, riboflavin, niacin, and pantothenic acid) are not adequately produced by the hindgut bacteria to accommodate the needs of an athlete. So if you have a horse that is working, training, or performing, you'll need to add more of these B vitamins. The best way to do so is to feed a B complex supplement. BPlex (Horsetech) offers all of the B vitamins without the added iron typically seen in B vitamin supplements.

Chapter Five

[10] If you have even a two month's hay supply, it's worth having it analyzed. However, if you are boarding your horse in a barn where the forage changes every week, getting an analysis is probably not feasible. In that case, you have the options of feeding it free choice without an analysis or soaking the hay to reduce detrimental sugar and starch.

Questions and Answers

[11] Getty, Juliet M., Ph.D., *Feed Your Horse Like A Horse*, 2010, page 235.

References

Ellis, A.D., and Hill, J. 2006. *Nutritional Physiology of the Horse*. United Kingdom: Nottingham University Press.

Getty, Juliet M., Ph.D. 2010. *Feed Your Horse Like a Horse*. Indianapolis, IN: Dog Ear Publishing.

Reed, S.M., Bayly, W.M., and Sellon, D.C. 2010. *Equine Internal Medicine*. Chapter 15: Disorders of the Gastrointestinal System. Pages 777-938. St. Louis, MO: Saunders Elsevier.

Riegel , R.J., and Hakola, W.E. 2007. *Illustrated Atlas of Clinical Equine Anatomy and Common Disorders of the Horse, Volume Two*. Chapter Five: The Digestive System. Pages 156-171. Marysville, Ohio: Equistar Publications, Limited.